A Year of Jewish Festivals

Flora York

FRANKLIN WATTS
LONDON•SYDNEY

First published in 2008
by Franklin Watts

Copyright © 2008 Franklin Watts

Franklin Watts
338 Euston Road
LONDON NW1 3BH

Franklin Watts Australia
Level 17/207 Kent Street
Sydney NSW 2000

Dewey classification: 296.4'3
ISBN: 978 0 7496 8342 9

Art Direction: Jonathan Hair
Illustrations: Peter Bull
Faith Consultant: Jonathan Gorsky

Designer (original edition): Joelle Wheelwright
Map (page 7): Aziz Khan
Picture Research: Diana Morris

Produced for Franklin Watts by Storeybooks.
The text of this book is based on *Jewish Festivals Through the Year* by Anita Ganeri
© Franklin Watts 2003.

Acknowledgements
The publishers would like to thank the following for permission to reproduce
photographs in this book:
Chris Fairclough/ Franklin Watts: 9t, 11; S. Grant/ Trip: 12t; I. Genut/ Trip: 16t,
20t, 20b, 23t; E. James/ Trip: 8b, 9b; Peter Millard/ Franklin Watts: 8t, 10b, 19b,
24; Muzlish/ Trip: 25t, 25b; © Palphot Ltd.: 10c; Zev Radovan, Jerusalem: front
cover, 7b, 15b; H. Rogers/ Trip: 14b, 18b, 19t, 22 (illustrations Heinz Sealig); R.
Seale/ Trip: 6b; S. Shapiro/ Trip: 21b; Steve Shott/ Franklin Watts: 17t, 26; J.
Soester/ Trip: 28c; A. Tovy/ Trip: 13b, 16b, 17b. Every attempt has been made to
clear copyright. Should there be any inadvertent omission please apply to the
publisher for rectification.

Printed in China

Franklin Watts is a division of Hachette Children's Books,
an Hachette Livre UK company.
www.hachettelivre.co.uk

Contents

Words printed in **bold** are explained in the glossary.

Jews

Jews are **descendants** of a people who lived in the Middle East a very long time ago. Their religion is called Judaism and is about 4,000 years old. Jews believe in God, and that God made our world.

Abraham

Abraham was the leader of the Hebrew people, who lived in the Middle East thousands of years ago.

Jews believe that God told Abraham that people who were descended from him would become a great nation.

Abraham's descendants became known as the Israelites, and later they were called the Jews.

▼ *The city of Jerusalem.*

Israel

God told Abraham that his descendants would have a land of their own, if they lived good lives. This Promised Land was Canaan (which we now call Israel). The capital of Israel is Jerusalem. It was here that the Jews built their first **Temple**.

The scattering

In the earliest times, Jewish people moved from place to place to find food, and land where their animals could graze. Sometimes, their enemies forced them to move to different parts of the Middle East.

In CE70, many Jews left their homeland and went to live all over Europe. This 'scattering' was known as the Diaspora.

Today, Jews live in many countries of the world, as well as in Israel.

The countries Jews live in today.

Israel

■ *The most Jews*
■ *Large numbers of Jews*
■ *Small numbers of Jews*
■ *Very small numbers of Jews*

▼ *Chatting to friends at a Jewish festival.*

Jewish festivals

A festival is a special day (or period of time) with its own **customs** and **ceremonies**. These may take place at home or in the **synagogue**. Most Jewish festivals mark things that happened in Jewish history.

Keeping Shabbat

Every week, Jews have a day of rest and prayer. It is called *Shabbat*, or the Sabbath, and lasts from dusk on Friday to Saturday night. People do not work on *Shabbat* and try to spend time with their family and friends. They also think about God and go to the synagogue.

◀ *On* Shabbat, *Jews eat a special loaf of bread made in the shape of a plait. It is called* challah.

Shabbat at home

On Friday evening, families have a special *Shabbat* meal. The mother lights candles to welcome the *Shabbat*. The father sings a prayer called the *Kiddush*, to thank God for *Shabbat*. Then the food is served.

◀ *The mother waves her hands over the candles to* **symbolise** *spreading joy and peace to the family.*

▲ *The **rabbi** helps people to understand the **Torah**.*

Synagogue service

On Saturday, there is a service in the synagogue led by a rabbi. The Torah **scroll** is taken out of the **Ark**. There are prayers, readings, and a talk by the rabbi.

Remembering

On *Shabbat*, Jews remember things that happened long ago.

They remember that God created the world in six days and rested on the seventh day. This day became *Shabbat*. (This is why Jews do not work on *Shabbat*.)

They remember the time when the Jewish people were slaves in Egypt. Eventually they escaped into the desert. God sent them food to eat. (*Challah* is a reminder of this.)

End of Shabbat

A ceremony called *Havdalah* marks the end of *Shabbat*. **Blessings** are said over wine, spices and a candle. Everyone sniffs the spices so that they can carry the scent of *Shabbat* into the next week.

◄ *The* Havdalah *ceremony is held at home and in the synagogue.*

Rosh Hashanah

The festival of *Rosh Hashanah* is the start of the Jewish New Year. People send cards and wish each other a happy new year, but this is also a serious time.

There are special services in the synagogue to help people think about the way that they behave. People say prayers, sing songs and listen to readings from the Torah.

◀ *Cards for* Rosh Hashanah.

Food at home

There is special food to enjoy during *Rosh Hashanah*. Apple dipped in honey, and honey cakes are popular. People share these sweet foods to wish each other a sweet and happy new year.

◀ *Slices of apple with honey for* Rosh Hashanah.

Ten important days

Rosh Hashanah is also the start of the Ten Days of **Penitence**. People think about their lives and ask God to forgive them for the wrong things that they have done during the year. They promise to do better. The Ten Days end with *Yom Kippur* (see page 13).

◀ *Blowing a shofar. In ancient times, this announced important events.*

The shofar

During the synagogue services, a musical instrument called a *shofar* is used. It is made out of a horn from a male sheep (ram).

The Torah says that the *shofar* must be blown at *Rosh Hashanah*.

The sound calls people to say sorry for the things that they have done wrong.

The curved shape of the horn is a reminder that life is not always straightforward.

Empty pockets

At *Rosh Hashanah*, some Jews go to a river or the sea to throw breadcrumbs or empty their pockets into the water. This symbolises God washing away the bad things they have done.

Jews in the USA collecting ▶
new year's resolutions
written on pieces of paper.

Make a Rosh Hashanah card

Make a *Rosh Hashanah* card for the Jewish New Year.

1. Fold a rectangle of card in half.

2. Decorate the card with Jewish symbols. You could draw a *shofar*, a six-pointed **Star of David**, or a scroll.

3. Write 'Leshanah Tovah' or 'Happy New Year' inside.

Scroll

Book

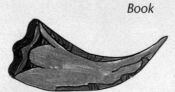

Shofar

Star of David

Yom Kippur

On the tenth Day of Penitence (see page 11), Jews ask God to forgive them for the wrong things they have done. This day is called *Yom Kippur*, or the Day of Atonement.

Marking Yom Kippur

Jews show God they are sorry for the bad things they have done by going without food and drink. This is called a fast. The fast at *Yom Kippur* lasts for about 25 hours.

There are services in the synagogue and many people wear white as a symbol of **purity**. The Torah scrolls are also covered in white cloth.

Saying sorry

On the night before *Yom Kippur*, Jews say sorry to people they have quarrelled with.

For Jews, *Yom Kippur* is the **holiest** day of the year.

They are very serious about saying sorry to God. They believe that if they really mean what they say, God will forgive them.

At the end of *Yom Kippur*, the *shofar* is blown. This is a sign that people can stop their fast.

Yom Kippur in Jerusalem. ▶ *Jews go to the Western Wall of the old Temple to pray.*

Sukkot

The festival of *Sukkot* is four days after *Yom Kippur*. It is a happy time after the serious thinking that takes place at *Yom Kippur*. *Sukkot* is called a **pilgrim festival**. In ancient times, all Jews would travel to Jerusalem to visit their holiest building, the Temple. *Sukkot* lasts for a week.

Remembering

At *Sukkot*, Jews remember when the Jewish people were slaves in Egypt. They finally escaped, then lived in the desert for many years before they reached the Promised Land.

God looked after them and kept them safe.

Harvest

In Israel, *Sukkot* traditionally marked the end of harvest time. This made it a harvest festival as well. People gave thanks for the food they had grown.

Children hanging ▶ *up pictures of fruit to celebrate* Sukkot.

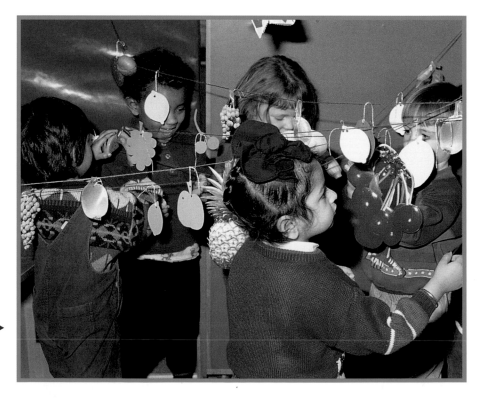

Huts

The word '*sukkot*' means 'huts'. For the festival, Jews may build a hut in the garden. It reminds them of the way the Jewish people lived in the desert after leaving Egypt.

The hut is usually built of wood. It has a roof of leaves or straw through which you can glimpse the sky and then think about God.

Jews eat their meals in the hut during Sukkot. *Some people even sleep there too.*

▼

Make a model hut

1. Make the roof frame by tying four sticks together with string to make a square.

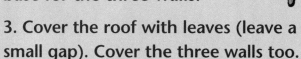

2. Fix a stick to each corner with string. These will hold the roof up. To strengthen the frame, fix three sticks around the base for the three walls.

3. Cover the roof with leaves (leave a small gap). Cover the three walls too. Decorate the hut with fruit made from card or modelling clay.

In the synagogue

There is a special service in the synagogue at *Sukkot*. Everyone holds branches and a citron (a fruit like a lemon).

During the service, people wave the branches while they sing. They also walk around and chant prayers that ask for God's help in their lives.

▲ *Waving branches during the* Sukkot *service spreads blessings over everyone.*

Plants for Sukkot

Four plants are used in the synagogue service. They stand for the parts of the body that can be used to worship God.

The plants give Jews guidelines for the way they should live.

The lulav *(date palm) stands for the back. Jews must walk tall and straight.*

Aravot *(willow leaves) stand for the mouth. Jews must speak truthfully.*

Hadassim *(myrtle leaves) stand for the eyes. Jews must see things clearly.*

The citron stands for the heart. Jews must make sure their heart is full of love and kindness.

Simchat Torah

This festival is straight after *Sukkot*. It **celebrates** the Torah.

The Torah is read in the synagogue every week. Readings start at the beginning of the Torah on *Simchat Torah* and finish a year later.

▼ Simchat Torah *in Jerusalem.*

The Torah

The Torah is the most holy part of the Jewish **scriptures**. It is about God and the Jewish people. It has many laws to follow.

The words are written on scrolls, which are kept in the Ark (a special cupboard) in the synagogue.

The Torah scrolls ▶ *are kept inside decorated covers.*

Parading the Torah

At *Simchat Torah*, the Torah scrolls are carried around the synagogue seven times. People walk behind, singing and dancing. Children wave flags, and jump to catch sweets thrown by the adults. The sweets are a symbol of the goodness of the Torah.

Hanukkah

Jews celebrate *Hanukkah* to remember a **miracle** that happened over 2,000 years ago. It showed people that God is always with them, even when their lives are difficult. The festival lasts for eight days in November or December.

The hanukiah ▶ *goes in the window so everyone can see it.*

Remembering

Long ago, invaders took over the Temple in Jerusalem and allowed the oil lamp there to go out. But some brave Jews drove them out.

When they tried to light the lamp again, there wasn't enough oil. But God kept the lamp burning for eight days, until the people could find more oil.

Candlelight

The *hanukiah* candlestick holds eight candles, plus another to light them with. The eight candles stand for the eight nights of *Hanukkah*. The number lit each night depends on which day of the festival it is. People say prayers and blessings before lighting each candle.

Fried foods

Jews eat foods fried in oil at *Hanukkah*. This reminds them of the oil in the Temple lamp. Families enjoy doughnuts and *latkes* (potato and onion pancakes).

Doughnuts are a ▶ *Hanukkah* treat.

Games

People like to play games during *Hanukkah*, such as *dreidel*.

A *dreidel* is a spinning top. On each side is a Hebrew letter. The letters are the initials of the words 'A great miracle happened there'.

The game may be played for raisins or chocolate coins. Each player spins the top. The letter it lands on is also an instruction. It tells the player to take all the raisins, take half, take none, or add one.

Dreidel *with six sides.*

A traditional dreidel *with four sides.*

19

Purim

The theme of *Purim* is good winning out over evil. The festival remembers the story of Esther in the Jewish Bible.

Purim is a happy time, with celebrations and fun for young and old.

Celebrations in the synagogue. ▶

Haman's pockets

There are special cakes to eat at *Purim*, called Haman's pockets. They are stuffed with honey, fruit and poppy seeds.

The story of Esther

The King of Persia's wife was called Queen Esther. He did not know that she was Jewish. Haman was the king's chief minister. He hated the Jews and decided to have them all killed.

Esther bravely told the king she was Jewish, and about Haman's plan. The king had Haman killed and the Jews were saved.

Purim service

There is a service at the synagogue, and the story of Esther is read out.

Whenever Haman is mentioned, everyone hisses and stamps their feet. They shake rattles called *greggors* to get rid of evil.

▼ *Israeli children wearing fancy dress at* Purim.

Make a greggor rattle

1. Find an empty soft drink can. Push some buttons, beads or beans through the pouring hole.

2. Cut a circle of cardboard to cover the end that has the hole. Glue in place.

3. Cut a felt circle for each end, and a piece of felt for the body of the can. Glue in place.

4. Cut felt shapes for decoration and glue them on.

Purim fun

Children go to *Purim* parties with games and dancing. There are also *Purim* plays and parades.

Adults and children often wear fancy dress at *Purim*. Sometimes they dress as people in the story of Esther.

Many people give money to charity at this time.

Pesach

This festival lasts for a week in March or April. *Pesach* is one of the most important times of the year for Jews.

They remember the time, long ago, when the Jewish people were slaves in Egypt and God helped them to escape. *Pesach* is also called Passover.

Moses

God told Moses to lead the Jewish people out of Egypt.

The ruler of Egypt was called the pharaoh. Moses asked the pharaoh to let the Jews go, but he refused. God sent ten **plagues** and then the pharaoh freed the Jewish people. They had been slaves for over 400 years.

Blood

Boils

Frogs

Hail

Lice

Locusts

Wild beasts

Darkness

Disease

Death of first-born sons

▲ *The ten plagues that affected the people of Egypt.*

A pilgrim festival

Pesach is a pilgrim festival. (*Sukkot* and *Shavuot* are also pilgrim festivals – see pages 14–16 and 26–27.) Long ago, all Jews would travel to Jerusalem for the pilgrim festivals. There they would visit the Temple, the most holy Jewish building.

▲ *Jewish children singing in the synagogue at* Pesach.

The Jewish people walk across the sea

Moses led the Jewish people into the desert. God showed them the way to go. A few days later, the pharaoh wished that he had not let the Jewish people go, and sent his army after them.

The Sea of Reeds

The Jewish people reached a big lake called the Sea of Reeds. But the Egyptian soldiers were behind them. The Jews were trapped!

God came to the rescue. God told Moses to stretch out his hand over the deep, rolling waters.

The waters part

As Moses stretched out his hand, the waters rolled away and a path of dry land appeared across the bed of the lake.

The Jews were able to cross the lake safely. But when the soldiers tried to follow them, the waters crashed back and drowned them all.

Food for Pesach

Families gather together at Pesach. They thank God for freeing the Jewish people from **slavery** thousands of years ago.

On the first night of Pesach, Jews eat foods that remind them of the life of the Jewish people in Egypt.

▼

Special seder plate.

Bitter herbs are reminders that slavery is horrible.

An egg and a lamb bone are like the offerings the Jewish people made to God.

Salty water is a symbol of the sweat and tears of the slaves.

A green vegetable is a sign of spring and new life.

Before Pesach

The family has to clean the house and get rid of foods made by leaving dough to rise, such as bread. This is a reminder of when the Jewish people had to leave Egypt so quickly that there was no time to let the bread dough rise, so the bread was flat.

Charoset *(nuts, apples and wine)* stands for the cement that the slaves used to make buildings for the Egyptians.

The seder

The meal on the first night of *Pesach* is called the *seder*. The youngest person asks four questions about the Jewish people's escape from slavery. Someone reads the answers from a book called the Haggadah. During this, people taste the foods on the *seder* plate, except for the egg and lamb bone.

◀ *The youngest person asks the four questions.*

Charoset

You will need:

2 apples
a handful of mixed nuts
a handful of raisins
a pinch of cinnamon
2 tablespoons grape juice

1. **Peel, core and chop or grate the apples.**

2. **Break up the nuts (put them in a plastic bag and crush with a rolling pin).**

3. **Mix all the ingredients together.**

Hunting for bread

Jews eat flat bread called *matzah* at *Pesach*. At the beginning of the *seder*, a piece (called the *afikomen*) is hidden in the room. After the meal, the children hunt for it. Mealtime does not end until it has been found. The finder gets a prize.

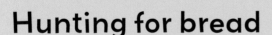

Matzah *at the* seder. ▶

Shavuot

When the Jewish people left Egypt, they wandered in the desert. After three months, they reached Mount Sinai. Moses went up the mountain to speak to God. Here, God gave Moses the Torah and the Ten Commandments.

The festival of *Shavuot* celebrates this time.

▲ *Reading from the Torah.*

The Ten Commandments

God spoke to Moses and gave him laws for the Jewish people to obey. This is what God said:

I am the Lord your God, who brought you out of Egypt, from slavery.

1. Do not worship any other god but me.
2. Do not make any statues or pictures to worship.
3. Do not use God's name wrongly.
4. Keep the *Shabbat* day holy.
5. Respect your parents.
6. Do not kill.
7. Do not be unfaithful to your husband or wife.
8. Do not steal.
9. Do not tell lies about others.
10. Do not be jealous of other people's possessions.

More about the Torah

The Torah is also called the Five Books of Moses, because Moses was given the first Torah by God.

The Torah tells how the world began. It gives the story of the lives of the first Jews. It contains many laws for Jews to follow.

There is a Torah in every synagogue. The words are written on **parchment**, in black ink. The sheets of parchment are sewn into a long piece. A wooden roller is attached to each end. This makes a scroll.

The Torah scrolls are kept inside covers, in a cupboard called the Ark.

Make a scroll

1. Write out a story on a long sheet of paper. (You could also use several sheets glued together.)

2. Find two long cardboard tubes and decorate the ends.

3. Glue each end of the paper to a tube. When the glue is dry, roll the paper on to the tubes.

4. Tie a coloured ribbon around the scroll. Unroll the scroll when you are ready to read.

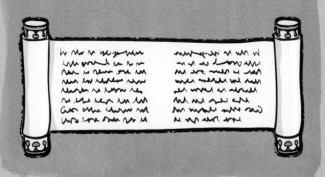

▲ *Putting flowers in the synagogue.*

In the synagogue

There are services at the synagogue for *Shavuot*. The story of the Ten Commandments is read from the Torah. The synagogue is decorated with flowers, because when the Torah was given to Moses, flowers came out on Mount Sinai.

Festival calendar

Date	Jewish month	Festival
1	Tishri	Rosh Hashanah
10	Tishri	Yom Kippur
15	Tishri	Sukkot
		Simchat Torah
25	Kislev	Hanukkah
14	Adar	Purim
15	Nisan	Pesach (Passover)
6	Sivan	Shavuot

Jewish months

The months of the Jewish year are:

Tishri	(September/October)
Heshvan	(October/November)
Kislev	(November/December)
Tevet	(December/January)
Sh'vat	(January/February)
Adar	(February/March)
Nisan	(March/April)
Iyyar	(April/May)
Sivan	(May/June)
Tamuz	(June/July)
Av	(July/August)
Elul	(August/September)

Glossary

Ark	A cupboard in the synagogue in which the Torah scrolls are kept.
Blessings	Special words said to thank or worship God, or make something holy. A blessing can also ask God to protect someone or something.
Celebrate	To be pleased and happy about something, and to have festivities to mark the occasion. These are called a celebration.
Ceremonies	Occasions where you do special things to mark an event.
Customs	Habits or traditions.
Descendants	People who are part of a family line. You are a descendant of your parents. They are descendants of their parents (your grandparents).
Holy, holiest	Something to do with God. A person who is holy is extremely good and dedicated to God.
Miracle	Something wonderful or amazing that happens, which is due to the power of God.
Parchment	Animal skin that is treated to make a material that can be written on.
Penitence	Being sorry about things that you have done wrong and putting them right.
Pilgrim festivals	The three Jewish festivals of *Pesach*, *Shavuot* and *Sukkot*. Pilgrims are people who go on a journey to visit a holy place.
Plague	A disease affecting many people. A 'plague' can also mean something that is an unpleasant nuisance.
Purity	The state of being pure – unspoilt, clean and good.
Rabbi	A Jewish teacher and leader in the synagogue.
Scriptures	Holy writings and books.
Scroll	A roll of parchment with writing on.
Slavery	Making people into slaves. The person who owns the slave controls the slave's life. The slave is forced to work for his or her owner.
Star of David	A six-pointed star, which has become a symbol of the Jews. It is named after a Jewish king called David.
Symbolise, symbol	To stand for something else; something that stands for something else.
Synagogue	A building in which Jews meet and worship.
Temple	The Temple was the ancient Jewish temple in Jerusalem. It was the holiest building for the Jews.
Torah	The holiest teachings of the Jews, written on a scroll. The Torah is also known as the Five Books of Moses.
Worship	To show love and respect for God.

Further resources

Websites

www.new-year.co.uk/jewish
Facts, background and activities for *Rosh Hashanah*.

www.akhlah.com
The Jewish Children's Learning Network. All aspects of Judaism.

www.torahtots.com/educmtrl. htm
Includes information on Jewish festivals and other aspects of Judaism.

www.hanukat.com
All about *Hanukkah* for Jewish and non-Jewish children.

Note to parents and teachers: Every effort has been made by the Publishers to ensure that these websites are suitable for children, that they are of the highest educational value, and that they contain no inappropriate or offensive material. However, because of the nature of the Internet, it is impossible to guarantee that the contents of these sites will not be altered. We strongly advise that Internet access is supervised by a responsible adult.

Index